TOTALLY CANADA

Puzzles, Games, Facts and Fun!

by
Jeff Sinclair

Scholastic Canada Ltd.

For Denise . . .
because she noticed!
— J.S.

National Library of Canada Cataloguing in Publication

Sinclair, Jeff
Totally Canada / Jeff Sinclair.

ISBN 0-439-96969-7

1. Canada — Miscellanea — Juvenile literature.
2. Puzzles — Juvenile literature.
3. Games — Juvenile literature. I. Title.

FC58.S58 2004   j971'.002   C2003-904902-7

6 5 4 3 2 1   Printed in Canada   04 05 06 07 08

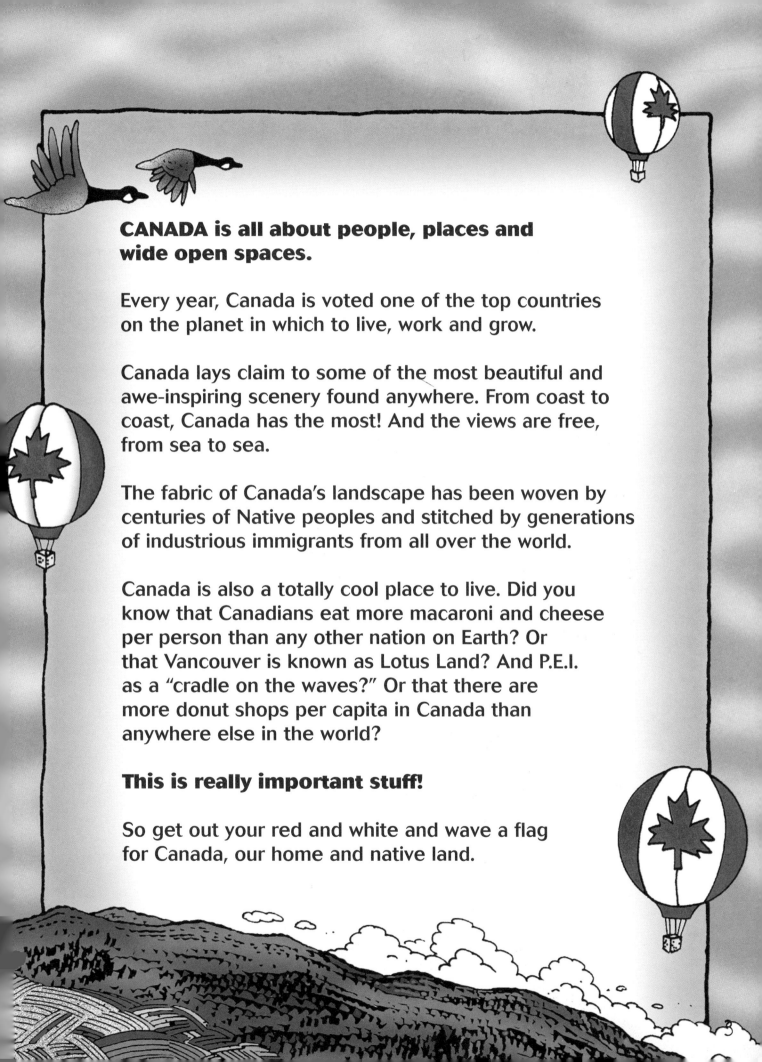

CANADA is all about people, places and wide open spaces.

Every year, Canada is voted one of the top countries on the planet in which to live, work and grow.

Canada lays claim to some of the most beautiful and awe-inspiring scenery found anywhere. From coast to coast, Canada has the most! And the views are free, from sea to sea.

The fabric of Canada's landscape has been woven by centuries of Native peoples and stitched by generations of industrious immigrants from all over the world.

Canada is also a totally cool place to live. Did you know that Canadians eat more macaroni and cheese per person than any other nation on Earth? Or that Vancouver is known as Lotus Land? And P.E.I. as a "cradle on the waves?" Or that there are more donut shops per capita in Canada than anywhere else in the world?

This is really important stuff!

So get out your red and white and wave a flag for Canada, our home and native land.

O Canada!
CANADA'S NATIONAL ANTHEM

O Canada! Our home and native land!
True patriot love in all thy sons command.
With glowing hearts we see thee rise,
The True North strong and free!
From far and wide, O Canada,
We stand on guard for thee.
God keep our land glorious and free!
O Canada, we stand on guard for thee.
O Canada, we stand on guard for thee.

O Canada! Terre de nos aïeux,
Ton front est ceint de fleurons glorieux!
Car ton bras sait porter l'épée,
Il sait porter la croix!
Ton histoire est une épopée
Des plus brillants exploits.
Et ta valeur, de foi trempée,
Protégera nos foyers et nos droits.
Protégera nos foyers et nos droits.

Music composed in 1880
by Calixa Lavallée

English lyrics written in 1908
by Robert Stanley Weir

French lyrics written in 1880
by Adolphe-Basile Routhier

Proclaimed Canada's
national anthem
in 1980

se the words below to fill in the lanks at right.

Canada

Flag   leaf

sugar

twice

red

The Maple Leaf Flag

Many historians agree that the maple leaf began to be used as a symbol for _____ during the 1700s.

In 1921, King George V proclaimed that the official colours of the royal arms of Canada were ___ and white.

In 1964, George Stanley, a professor at the Royal Military College in Kingston, Ontario, suggested a one-leaf design for Canada's national flag. He wrote, "The single ___ has the virtue of simplicity. It emphasizes the distinct Canadian symbol and suggests a loyalty to a single country."

Although many kinds of maple trees grow in Canada, a _____ maple leaf was chosen as the basis for the flag's leaf design.

The Canadian flag is _____ as long as it is wide.

On February 15, 1965, by proclamation of Her Majesty, Queen Elizabeth II, Canada's newest national symbol came into use across the country and around the world. February 15 is now officially recognized as National ___ of Canada Day.

Answers on page 45

5

Sea-to-Sea Scavenger Hunt

Search the pages of *Totally Canada* for the 20 items found on the scavenger list below. These Canadian collector pieces may be anywhere and on any page. A few appear *twice!*

Answers on page 45

Found on page:

1. **campfire** _____
2. **Saddledome** _____
3. **bunch of wheat** _____
4. **Albertosaurus dinosaur** _____
5. **moose in a Mountie hat** _____
6. **pine cone** _____
7. **Parliament Buildings** _____
8. **goalie stick** _____
9. **porcupine** _____
10. **turkey on rye** _____
11. **snapping turtle** _____
12. **maple leaf mug** _____
13. **beaver on a totem pole** _____
14. **bear with a toothache** _____
15. **hot air balloon** _____
16. **Canadian quarter** _____
17. **octopus** _____
18. **lobster in a box** _____
19. **bucket of fish** _____
20. **Canada goose holding a flag** _____

CANADA QUIZ: Which of the Great Lakes is totally NOT in Canada? _____

Answer on page 45

FAMOUS CANADIANS

5 ALL-TIME GREATS: Can you name them?

1. In 1534, the first European to explore the St. Lawrence River, and to put the word "Canada" on a map: _____

2. In 1867, the first Prime Minister of Canada: _____

3. The discoverer of insulin, and co-winner of the 1923 Nobel Prize in medicine: _____

4. The young man who set out to run across Canada to raise funds for cancer research: _____

5. In 1992, Canada's first female astronaut: _____

Answers on page 45

AUTHORS

1. Margaret Atwood
2. Pierre Berton
3. Gordon Korman
4. Jean Little
5. L.M. Montgomery
6. Farley Mowat
7. Robert Munsch

ARTISTS

1. Robert Bateman
2. Emily Carr
3. Alex Colville
4. Kenojuak
5. Jean-Paul Riopelle
6. Tom Thomson
7. The Group of Seven

SPORTS STARS

1. Wayne Gretzky
2. Catriona LeMay Doan
3. Mario Lemieux
4. David Pelletier and Jamie Salé
5. Jacques Villeneuve
6. Mike Weir
7. Hayley Wickenheiser

MOVIE STARS

1. Jim Carrey
2. Hayden Christensen
3. Mike Myers
4. Catherine O'Hara
5. Martin Short
6. Kiefer Sutherland

EXPLORERS

1. John Cabot
2. Samuel de Champlain
3. Captain James Cook
4. Sir Alexander Mackenzie
5. David Thompson
6. Sir John Franklin
7. Henry Kelsey

MUSIC STARS

1. Barenaked Ladies
2. Céline Dion
3. Nelly Furtado
4. Avril Lavigne
5. Sarah McLachlan
6. Nickelback
7. Shania Twain

7

WET 'N' WILD HINK PINKS

Here's a kooky collection of aquatic Hink Pinks fished from Canada's coastlines — from the waters of the Strait of Georgia to the Bay of Fundy. Hink Pinks are 2 rhyming one-syllable words like Fish Wish and Fake Lake. You'll catch on quick.

Answers on page 45

1 A fish using counterfeit money is committing ...

6 A soggy heap on the dock is a ...

2 Two belugas for the price of one is a ...

7 When you cram a load of herring into a phone booth, you ...

3 A boring seabird is a ...

8 A bucket of fish makes a tasty ...

4 The 'ink squirter's offspring are the ...

9 A mollusc in trouble with the law is in a ...

5 A fearless farewell is a ...

10 An overweight crustacean should lose some ...

COUNTRY-WIDE WORD SCRAMBLE

You could go totally squirrelly figuring out these 20 jumbled-up Canadian people, places and things. Each is mentioned or can be seen somewhere in the book. Some of them are easy, but others may drive you nutty!

Answers on page 45

1. TROBER CHUMNS _____
2. BLUMAP _____
3. CORKY SNIATUNMO _____
4. RIPEER UTRUADE _____
5. TARGE AKELS _____
6. PLEAM FLEA _____
7. BLOOSINEWM _____
8. TS. ENCLAWRE IVRRE _____
9. RIPNEC DEDWAR DILSNA _____
10. VEEBAR _____

11. NUMTO OLGNA _____
12. IBCAORU _____
13. TIUNI _____
14. NGERE AGBELS _____
15. GLCILM IVRYSNUITE _____
16. MPAEL YSUPR _____
17. MRPC _____
18. NAWHECKATSSA _____
19. UEMASL ED CAMHNPLIA _____
20. LEANSTY PCU _____

CANADA QUIZ: What percentage of Canada's land is covered by forests and woods? _____

Answer on page 45

10

Moose grow heavy horns on their heads called antlers. They shed these antlers every year and grow a new pair. Each antler looks like a large cupped hand with finger-like points. The TRUE McKenzie Moose hiding in these wooded pages has 5 points on each antler. When you spot him, give out your best moose call!

Answer on page 45

Crazy Canada

There are 10 items in this crazy Canadian scene that are trying to pass themselves off as being native to Canada. But they are really imports from other places around the world. Try to find all 10 in 60 seconds or less. Colour in the scene, and then report them all to Canada Customs!

Answers on page 45

BARKY BEAVER'S OTTAWA EXPEDITION

Barky Beaver is on his way to Ottawa to visit the Parliament Buildings. But he is a-MAZE-d at just how many different routes he can take to get there. You can give Barky a hand by getting out your pencil and marking a path for him to follow.

Solution on page 45

ACROSS CANADA

Are you ready to take a trip across Canada? Starting out in Vancouver, make your way across the country by rolling one or two dice. If you land on a square where a flagpole's been planted, shinny up to reach the Canadian flag. Land at the end of a hockey stick and you slide down to serve your penalty. The first person to make it to St. John's has made it across Canada.

CANADA QUIZ: Toronto's international airport is

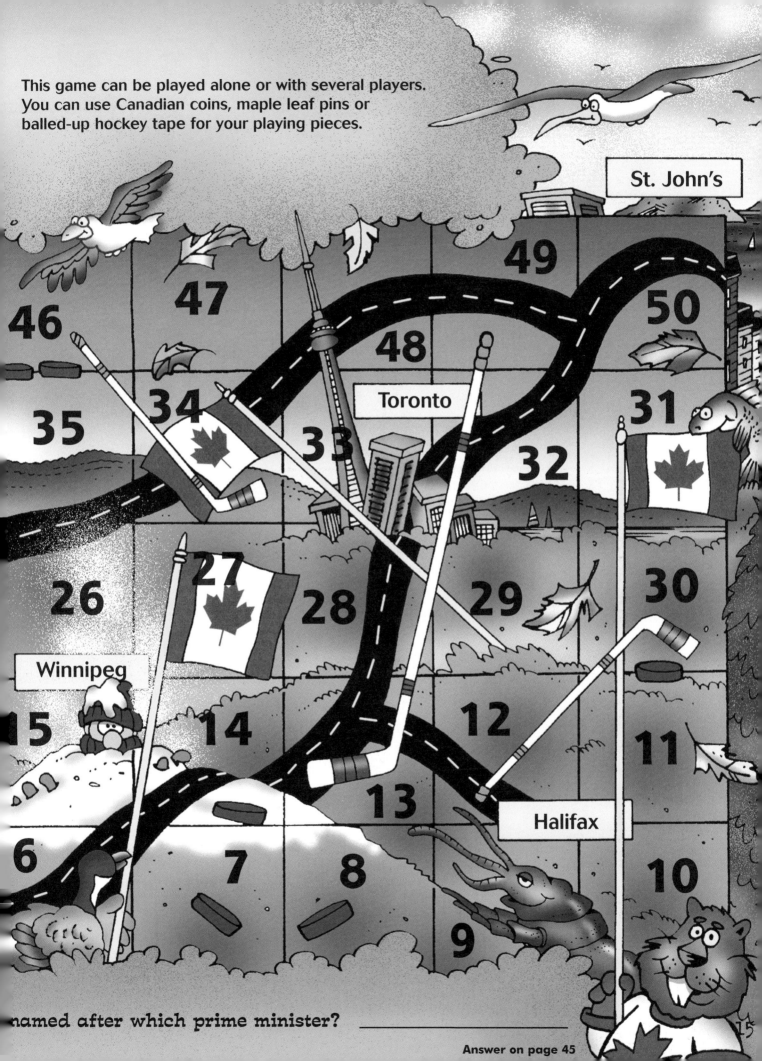

This game can be played alone or with several players. You can use Canadian coins, maple leaf pins or balled-up hockey tape for your playing pieces.

named after which prime minister? _____

Answer on page 45

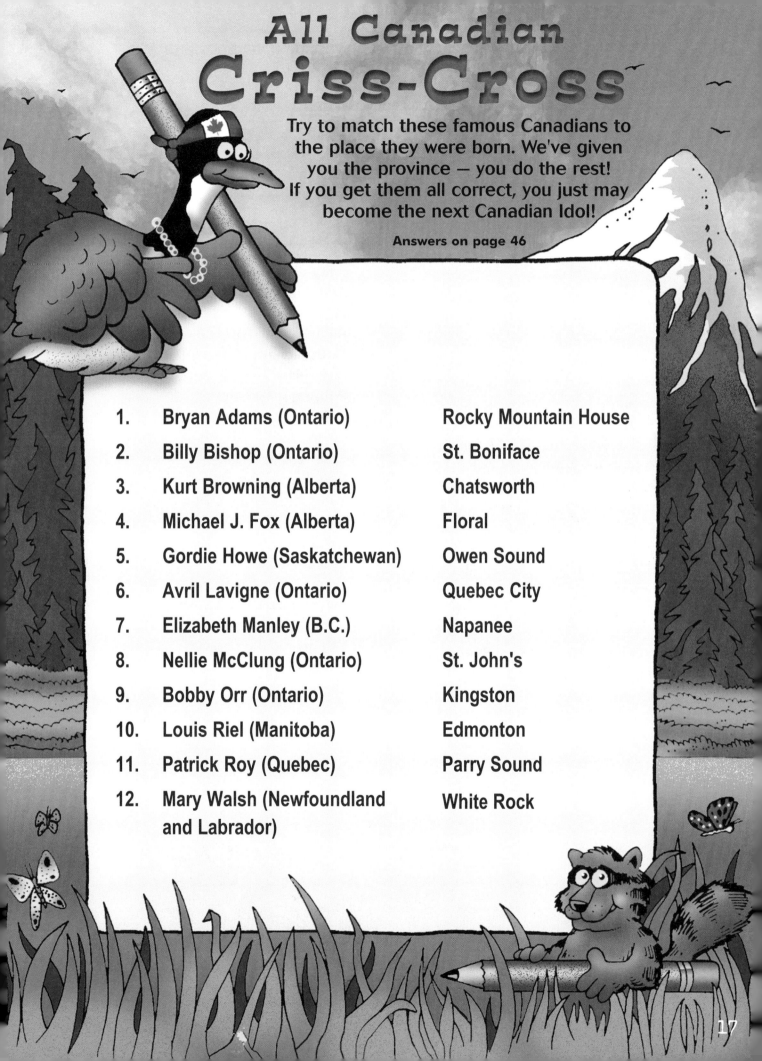

All Canadian Criss-Cross

Try to match these famous Canadians to the place they were born. We've given you the province — you do the rest! If you get them all correct, you just may become the next Canadian Idol!

Answers on page 46

1.	Bryan Adams (Ontario)	Rocky Mountain House
2.	Billy Bishop (Ontario)	St. Boniface
3.	Kurt Browning (Alberta)	Chatsworth
4.	Michael J. Fox (Alberta)	Floral
5.	Gordie Howe (Saskatchewan)	Owen Sound
6.	Avril Lavigne (Ontario)	Quebec City
7.	Elizabeth Manley (B.C.)	Napanee
8.	Nellie McClung (Ontario)	St. John's
9.	Bobby Orr (Ontario)	Kingston
10.	Louis Riel (Manitoba)	Edmonton
11.	Patrick Roy (Quebec)	Parry Sound
12.	Mary Walsh (Newfoundland and Labrador)	White Rock

MADE IN CANADA

Check out all the awesome inventions that have their origins in Canada. It's a remarkable list of what Canada has contributed to the world.

911 CPR dummy — Dianne Croteau, Richard Brault and Jonathan Vinden

Anti-gravity suit — Dr. Wilbur R. Franks

Avro Arrow — Royal Canadian Air Force

Basketball — Dr. James A. Naismith

Chocolate bar — James K. Ganong

Electric cooking range — Thomas Ahearn

Electric wheelchair — George J. Klein

Electron microscope — University of Toronto

Five-pin bowling — Thomas E. Ryan

Football goalpost with single base — Jim Trimble

Fuller brush — Alfred C. Fuller

Ginger ale — John J. McLaughlin

Green garbage bag — Harry Wasylyk

Green ink — Thomas Sterry Hunt

Hydrofoil boat — Casey Baldwin and Alexander Graham Bell

Imax film format — Grahame Ferguson, Roman Kroitor and Robert Kerr

Insulin — Dr. Frederick Banting

Java programming language — James Gosling

Jolly Jumper — Olivia Poole

Kerosene — Dr. Abraham Gesner

Light bulb — Henry Woodward (later sold the patent to Thomas Edison)

McIntosh apple — John McIntosh

Newsprint — Charles Fenerty

Pablum — Doctors T.G.H. Drake, Alan Brown and Frederick F. Tisdall

Pacemaker — Wilfred Bigelow

Paint roller — Norman Breakey

Panoramic camera — John Cannon

Snow blower — Arthur Sicard

Snowmobile — Joseph-Armand Bombardier

Standard Time — Sir Sandford Fleming

Superman — Joe Shuster

Synchronized swimming — Canadian Royal Lifesaving Society

Telegraph — Frederic Newton Gesborne

Telephone — Alexander Graham Bell

Trivial Pursuit — Chris Haney and Scott Abbott

Velcro — George de Mestral

Walkie-Talkie — Donald L. Hings

Zipper — Gideon Sundback

METRIC MANIA

Canada officially adopted the metric system of measurement in 1970. But it was not until January of 1975 that product labelling in metric began.

Take this Metric Multiple-Choice Quiz to test your mastery of metric!

Answers on page 46

1 What's the temperature of a bear's nose?
a) 32°C   b) 100°C   c) 0°C

2 How much water do you need for a load of laundry?
a) 15.0 L
b) 150 L
c) 82.5 L

3 How heavy is a bag of flour?
a) 10 kg
b) 2.5 g
c) 525 000 g

4 What's the length of a newborn baby?
a) 1250 mm
b) 50 cm
c) .85 m

5 How much milk is in a jug?
a) 1000 g
b) 4 L
c) 40 mL

6 How beefy is a prime Alberta steer?
a) 400 kg
b) 50 000 L
c) 800 cm

7 What's the area of an average bedroom door?
a) 6 sq m
b) 2600 sq cm
c) 1.6 sq m

CANADA QUIZ: How many Canadian provinces share a border with Alaska? _____
Answer on page 46

19

Do You C What I C?

You must be **C**-ing things — a lot of things that start with the totally **C**anadian letter **C**, in fact. Even if they're not **C**anadian, they still **C**ount! **C** if you **C**an find all 25 of them. Then **C**olour them in!

Answers on page 46

Get Cookin' Canada!

Match each of these delightful dishes to their province or territory, and you've got a recipe for fun!

Then turn up the heat and match them to one or more food groups from Canada's Food Guide to Healthy Eating — maybe all 4!

A) Grain Products
B) Vegetables and Fruit
C) Milk Products
D) Meat and Alternatives

Answers on page 46

Surrey Smoked Salmon

1 _____

Bonnyville Beef 'n' Broccoli

2 _____

Iqaluit Caribou Burger

4 _____

Mount Logan Lasagna

3 _____

Saskatoon Berry Loaf

7 _____

Selkirk Sunflower Salad

6 _____

Timmins Turkey on Rye

5 _____

Beaupré Baked Beans

8 _____

Caraquet Carrot Sticks

Annapolis Apples and Cheese

10 _____

Corner Brook Cod with Cabbage

Yellowknife Yogurt with Blueberries

9 _____

Charlottetown Spuds with Sour Cream

11 _____

13 _____

12 _____

21

All-Canadian Quotes

"O sweet Canada, Canada, Canada!"

"It is wonderful to feel the grandness of Canada in the raw, not because she is Canada but because she's something sublime that you were born into, some great rugged power that you are a part of."

— Emily Carr

"If you don't think that your country should come before yourself, you can better serve your country by livin' someplace else."

— Stompin' Tom Connors

"Canada is the linchpin of the English-speaking world."

— Sir Winston Churchill

"When I'm in Canada, I feel this is what the world should be like."

— Jane Fonda

"Our hopes are high. Our faith in the people is great. Our courage is strong. And our dreams for this beautiful country will never die."

— Pierre Trudeau

"I am a Canadian, free to speak without fear, free to worship in my own way, free to stand for what I think right, free to oppose what I believe wrong, or free to choose those who shall govern my country. This heritage of freedom I pledge to uphold for myself and all mankind."

— John Diefenbaker

"There are no limits to the majestic future which lies before the mighty expanse of Canada with its virile, aspiring, cultured and generous-hearted people."

— Sir Winston Churchill

"I am so excited about Canadians ruling the world."

— John Diefenbaker

"I don't even know what street Canada is on."

— Al Capone

"In a world darkened by ethnic conflicts that tear nations apart, Canada stands as a model of how people of different cultures can live and work together in peace, prosperity and mutual respect."

— Bill Clinton

CANADA QUIZ: Which 2 animals appear on the Canadian coat of arms? _____ and _____

Answers on page 46

The Totally Canada Trivia Challenge Part 1

1. What do Canadians eat more of than any other nation on Earth?
   a) peanut butter and banana sandwiches   b) macaroni and cheese   c) crow

2. In Canada's national anthem, Canada is referred to as . . .
   a) the place with a lot of trees   b) sweet land of liberty
   c) the True North strong and free

3. February 15 is recognized in Canada as . . .
   a) Flag Day   b) Groundhog Day   c) just another day in paradise

4. One of Canada's most well-known authors is . . .
   a) Hardley Knowit   b) Barley Sowit   c) Farley Mowat

5. The REAL McKenzie Moose has what on his antlers?
   a) a satellite dish   b) 5 points   c) duct tape

6. Avril Lavigne comes from what town in Ontario?
   a) Tricknee   b) Slapmynee   c) Napanee

7. Name the Canadian product that John J. McLaughlin invented.
   a) ginger ale   b) bathroom scale   c) roofing nail

8. Victoria, B.C. has the lowest what in Canada?
   a) annual snowfall   b) ceilings   c) self-esteem

9. Who said "I don't even know what street Canada is on"?
   a) Weird Al Yankovic   b) Al Bundy   c) Al Capone

10. In January 1975, Canada began labelling products . . .
    a) in Klingon   b) in metric   c) in order to confuse the masses

TOTALLY CANADA CROSSWORD

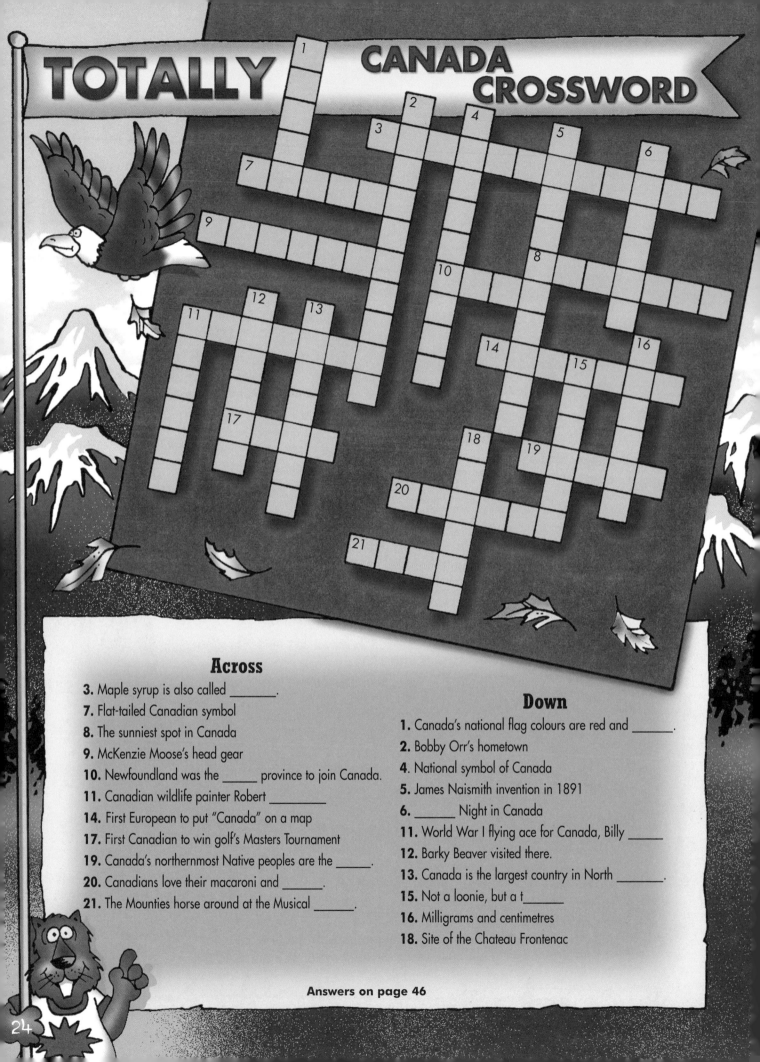

Across

3. Maple syrup is also called _____.

7. Flat-tailed Canadian symbol

8. The sunniest spot in Canada

9. McKenzie Moose's head gear

10. Newfoundland was the _____ province to join Canada.

11. Canadian wildlife painter Robert _____

14. First European to put "Canada" on a map

17. First Canadian to win golf's Masters Tournament

19. Canada's northernmost Native peoples are the _____.

20. Canadians love their macaroni and _____.

21. The Mounties horse around at the Musical _____.

Down

1. Canada's national flag colours are red and _____.

2. Bobby Orr's hometown

4. National symbol of Canada

5. James Naismith invention in 1891

6. _____ Night in Canada

11. World War I flying ace for Canada, Billy _____

12. Barky Beaver visited there.

13. Canada is the largest country in North _____.

15. Not a loonie, but a t_____

16. Milligrams and centimetres

18. Site of the Chateau Frontenac

Answers on page 46

24

Weather OR NOT!

Go anywhere in Canada and you can bet you'll find people talking about the weather. From its highs to its lows, from the rain to the snow, Canada has some of the most diverse weather on Earth.

Victoria, B.C. has the lowest average annual snowfall at 47 cm.

Lakelse Lake, B.C. recorded the heaviest snowfall in one day — 118.1 cm — on January 17, 1974.

Chicoutimi, Quebec holds the record for the most number of days per year with blowing snow at 37. *Brrrr!!*

Yellowknife, Northwest Territories records the coldest winters in Canada, with average nighttime temperatures during the months of December, January and February dropping to a bone-chilling –30.0˚ Celsius.

Winnipeg, Manitoba boasts the sunniest winters with the most hours of sunshine during December, January and February — a total of 358 hours.

Kamloops, B.C. can brag about the warmest summers in Canada with an average daytime temperature of 27.2˚ Celsius during June, July and August. Bring your swim trunks!

Vancouver, B.C. is the city with the fewest days below freezing, with an average of a mere 51 days per year with freezing temperatures.

The lowest temperature recorded in Canada is –63˚ Celsius at **Snag, Yukon Territory** on February 3, 1947.

Corner Brook, Newfoundland is the snowiest city in Canada with an annual average snowfall of 414 cm.

Medicine Hat, Alberta claims the title of Canada's Driest City, with 271 days without measurable precipitation.

Estevan, Saskatchewan is the Sunshine Capital of Canada, with the greatest number of hours of sunlight per year — a whopping 2500 hours.

Windsor, Ontario is Canada's most humid city with the highest average vapour pressure — 1.78 kilopascals — during June, July and August.

Prince Rupert, B.C. is the wettest place in Canada, with a total annual precipitation of 2552 mm. Surf's up, dudes!

CANADA QUIZ: The largest hailstone ever documented in Canada fell in Saskatchewan. It was as big as a) a golf ball b) a tennis ball c) a softball _____

Answer on page 46

Kooky Canuck Alphabet Adventure

Fill in the missing letters to these 20 totally Canadian people, places and things. Then use the circled letters to unscramble the hidden message.

PEOPLE

1. _ ERR _ _ OX

2. ○HAN _ _ _ WA _ N

3. RO _ E _ T B○TEMA _

4. _ _RT _ N BR _ DEU _

PLACES

5. MO _ C _ ON

6. Q _ EBE _ ©_ _Y

7. MAN _ TO _ _

8. N _ ○AV _ T

9. N _ W _ OU _ _ L _ NⒹ

10. _ _ MM _ NS

THINGS

11. _ACK B _ _ ON

12. _ LBE _ TOS _ _Ⓡ_ S

13. B _ S _ ET _ _ LⓁ

14. C _ N _ Ⓔ

15. PO _ _ R B _ _ R

16. _ _ NG _ R _ ○LE

17. I _ E _ _ CK _ _

18. _ LU _ J_Y

19. NAN○_ MO _ AR

20. I _ UK _ Ⓤ_

Hidden Message:
○○○○○○ ○○○○○!

Answers on page 46

26

Funny Money

Canada has some of the coolest looking currency in the world. But can you tell which bill is which, just by looking at its artsy side? Give yourself a toonie if you identify them all!

Do you know what's on the other side of each Canadian coin?

6) penny _____   7) nickel _____

8) dime _____   9) quarter _____

10) loonie _____   11) toonie _____

Answers on page 46

Take a Hike Hinkie Pinkies

Trekking through the Canadian wilderness is an awesome adventure. As you hike along the tree-lined trails, try these hilarious Hinkie Pinkies (two rhyming 2-syllable words).

Answers on page 47

1 A dam builder's kitchen knife is a ...

2 A biting turtle who loves hip hop is a ...

3 If you live alone in a cave, you'll need a ...

4 A flower that can't be bothered to bloom is a ...

5 A bear with a toothache has a sore ...

6 A foul Thanksgiving fowl is a ...

7 A cascading waterfall is a ...

8 A giant B.C. conifer free of insects is a ...

CANADA QUIZ: What is the longest river in Canada? _____

Answer on page 47

Maple Syrup Canadian Gold

Centuries before any European explorers arrived in Canada, Native peoples of the eastern woodlands had perfected the art of drawing off maple sap from the sugar maple tree and boiling it down to make sugar.

Each spring, Native peoples would slice the bark of the tree trunks with a tomahawk and wedge in a wooden chip to funnel the sap into a birchbark container. Then they would steam the sap in hollowed logs or clay pots, until all that remained was the maple sugar.

As settlers arrived from France, and then from elsewhere in Europe, Native peoples taught them the art of tapping the maples.

Today, although maple trees are tapped in a handful of American states, Canada is king, producing 85% of the world's maple syrup. And which province supplies almost all of that? The province of Quebec is far and away the top producer of maple syrup and maple products in the world.

For many Québécois, spring would not be spring without a time-honoured visit to *la cabane à sucre* — the sugar shack!

A 10-minute misconduct penalty has been given to Barky Beaver for the illegal use of a hockey stick to build a dam at centre ice. See if you can spot the 10 missing, added or changed items in the rink on the right. Scoring all 10 may get your name on the Stanley Cup!

Answers on page 47

THE ROYAL CANADIAN MOUNTED POLICE

The Musical Ride

The Musical Ride was developed by early members of the North West Mounted Police to entertain the local community and to display their riding abilities. Since many of them came from British military backgrounds, it is not surprising that the Musical Ride is based on traditional cavalry drill moves.

Today the horses are bred in Canada at the breeding farm in Pakenham, Ontario. They are all black, weigh between 523 kg and 635 kg, stand 16 to 17 hands high and are predominately Thoroughbred. Approximately 10 horses are moved in their third year to the RCMP Training Facility and Stables in Ottawa. At the age of 6, about half of these graduate to the Musical Ride.

The horse, the scarlet tunic and the lance that are displayed in the Musical Ride are the few remaining links to the RCMP's early history.

The NWMP Timeline

The North West Mounted Police force was conceived by Sir John A. Macdonald, first Prime Minister of Canada and Minister of Justice, and established by an Act of Parliament in 1873.

The motto of the police force was *Maintiens le droit*. These French words, meaning "Uphold the Right," stood to ensure that peace, justice and order were maintained in the Canadian west.

From 1874-1905, the role of the NWMP was to patrol and enforce the laws in the prairie region, establish friendly relations with the Native peoples and assist in the settlement of new immigrants and pioneers.

The Mounted Police expanded their jurisdiction into the Yukon in 1895 and to the Arctic coast, in 1903. The now "Royal" NWMP were contracted to police the area of Alberta and Saskatchewan in 1905, and northern Manitoba in 1912. In 1920, the police force was reorganized and the RNWMP became the Royal Canadian Mounted Police.

The Mounties' Stetson

In their early history, the NWMP wore either pillbox caps or pith helmets made of cork covered in cloth. But by the late 1800s, many officers went out on patrol wearing felt prairie or cowboy hats. Because of the weather conditions in western Canada, these made a much more practical head covering. In 1901, the NWMP adopted the famous brown felt Stetson, originally made by the John B. Stetson Company, as part of their standard dress. Today, the Stetson hat is made with loving care by Biltmore, a Canadian company.

COAST-TO-COAST
Canadian Landmarks

In what province is each of these famous Canadian landmarks located? Watch out — one of the answers is tricky!

Answers on page 47

1 Canada Place

2 Saddledome

3 Citadel Clock

4 Chateau Frontenac

5 Green Gables

6 Confederation Bridge

7 CN Tower

Canada-Wide

Canada is a pretty wide country, and this
Canada-wide word search covers it all!

M	A	P	L	E	L	E	A	F	C	L	E	S	L	B	I	T	L	P
R	G	B	O	D	E	C	K	V	P	D	E	G	C	A	R	E	K	E
C	T	L	S	R	P	I	T	T	E	K	H	O	Y	A	V	S	I	E
A	Y	U	C	S	G	H	B	S	A	C	E	E	V	C	N	O	D	F
R	B	E	R	D	K	Y	E	L	S	H	A	S	T	U	N	O	D	S
I	T	N	K	C	K	P	T	C	K	A	U	E	E	R	K	G	E	C
B	I	O	A	Z	D	A	G	H	S	R	A	M	C	L	B	A	C	G
O	A	S	T	P	E	L	T	O	U	L	D	I	A	I	S	D	O	T
U	C	E	D	R	V	I	G	A	P	O	A	T	L	N	L	A	C	C
O	R	Y	G	P	B	C	S	E	Y	T	V	I	U	G	I	N	S	H
G	E	C	L	V	B	O	P	C	H	T	I	R	C	R	U	A	P	A
Y	V	R	O	U	T	A	Y	A	L	E	C	A	P	R	D	C	A	N
C	A	P	C	R	E	D	N	G	S	T	E	M	S	E	O	G	D	P
U	E	T	E	I	N	S	L	T	E	O	H	A	C	P	B	P	C	L
I	B	B	S	H	E	S	K	V	I	W	E	T	S	S	Y	A	L	A
C	L	D	O	E	N	A	I	D	A	N	A	C	M	A	I	O	T	I
A	U	L	A	Y	O	C	S	B	C	K	G	P	U	G	R	I	A	N

ALBERTOSAURUS	CANADA GOOSE	CHARLOTTETOWN	GASPÉ
BANTING	CANADIAN	CORN	GREAT LAKES
BEAVER	CANOE	CREE	GRETZKY
BEEF	CARIBOU	CURLING	MAPLE LEAF
BLUENOSE	CHAMPLAIN	DONUTS	MARITIMES

34

Word Search

Solution on page 46

Discover 40 Canadian people, places and things hiding horizontally, vertically, diagonally or even backwards!

```
C F R M O U N T I E S S E I R I A R P
I N W I G A T L K I S L O N L G F R Y
R L S T A N L E Y C U P A C F K I H W
T K L Y K E M O D E L D D A S M O P A
E C F G Y E L L O W K N I F E N S A B
M A N Y H A T H L B O Y L M G I T R A
T H E L E C O A F E D G I R A A W L L
F S L O D K T H L P M N A B M W S I A
C R O N N S R I F H I A A N O T M A I
A P I K M B U S S B I T P S A F M R
A G M L A O H R T E N S L R A I K E O
U E L M M N E F I G M Y O D N S N T
S T W Y D R O W K S I A I F A E T C
B O N A R T F I C L T A C T H G E I
N T H N P L A P O P H B F B S N P V
C H T R O N E U R T H A B D A C H T
B I D F A B T A H E N I C I D E M R
```

MEDICINE HAT	NAPANEE	SADDLEDOME	TOTEM POLE
METRIC	PARLIAMENT	SHANIA TWAIN	TRUE NORTH
MOOSE	PRAIRIES	SNOWMOBILE	TURKEY
MOUNTIES	PRIME MINISTER	STANLEY CUP	VICTORIA
NAISMITH	ROCKIES	SUGAR SHACK	YELLOWKNIFE

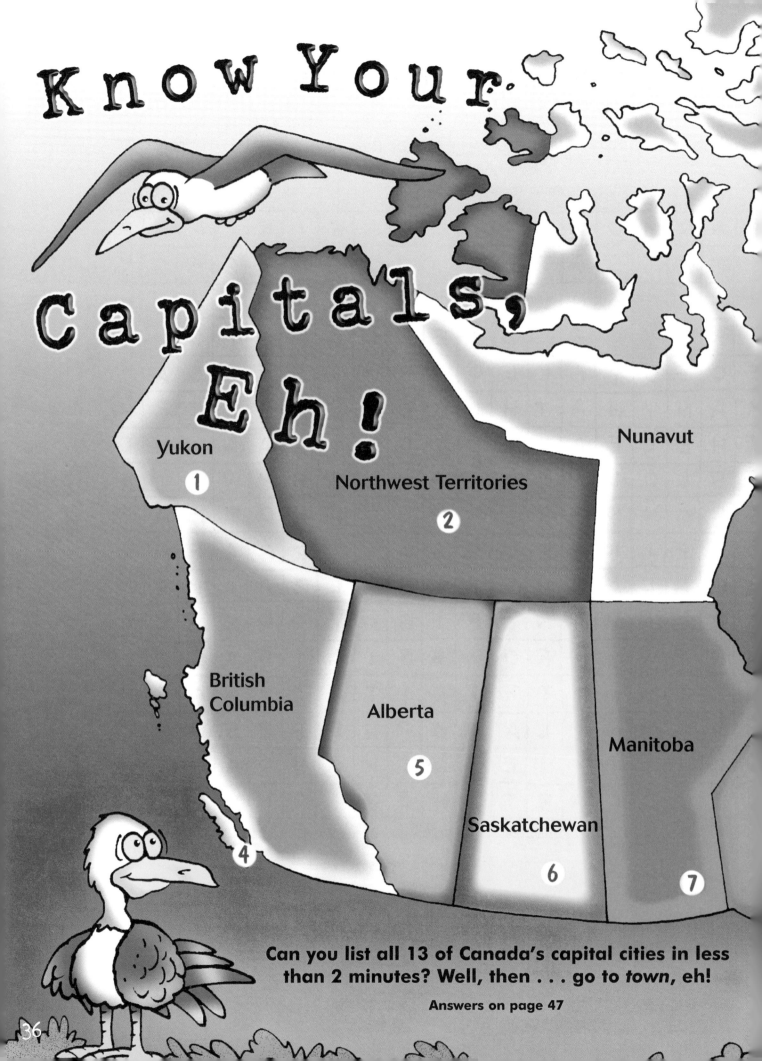

Know Your Capitals, Eh!

Yukon ①

Northwest Territories ②

Nunavut

British Columbia

Alberta ⑤

Saskatchewan ⑥

Manitoba ⑦

④

Can you list all 13 of Canada's capital cities in less than 2 minutes? Well, then . . . go to *town*, eh!

Answers on page 47

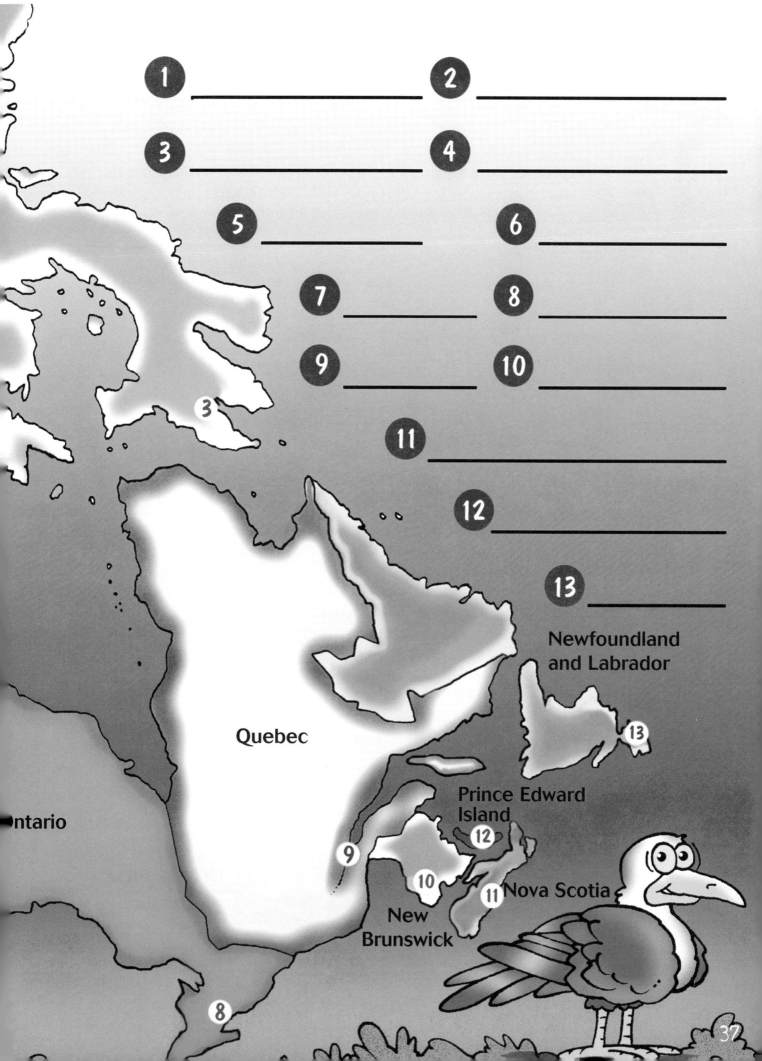

1 _____ 2 _____

3 _____ 4 _____

5 _____ 6 _____

7 _____ 8 _____

9 _____ 10 _____

11 _____

12 _____

13 _____

Newfoundland
and Labrador

Quebec

ntario

Prince Edward
Island

New
Brunswick

Nova Scotia

What's in a Name

Did you know that the word Canada comes from *kanata*,
the Huron word for settlement or village?

For centuries, Native peoples have lived on this great land in harmony with nature.
Today many places in Canada carry the names bestowed on them by various Aboriginal
groups. Here are the fascinating meanings and origins of a few of them.

Athabasca	where there are reeds	Cree
Chicoutimi	the end of the water	Montagnais
Coquitlam	small red salmon	Salish
Etobicoke	the place where the alders grow	Ojibwa
Gaspé	end or extremity	Mi'kmaq
Inuvik	the place of man	Inuit
Iqaluit	place of many fish	Inuit
Keewatin	north wind	Cree
Lillooet	wild onion	Lillooet
Nanaimo	big strong people	Salish
Nipigon	continuous water	Ojibwa
Oromocto	good river	Maliseet
Oshawa	crossing of stream	Seneca
Ottawa	to trade	Algonquin
Penticton	the always place	Okanagan
Saguenay	water flows out	Algonquin
Shubenacadie	the place where groundnuts (potatoes) grow	Mi'kmaq
Toronto	a place of meeting	Huron
Wetaskiwin	place of peace	Cree
Winnipeg	murky water	Cree

Ever heard of TOPONYMY?
It's the study of the place names of a region.
You're doing it!

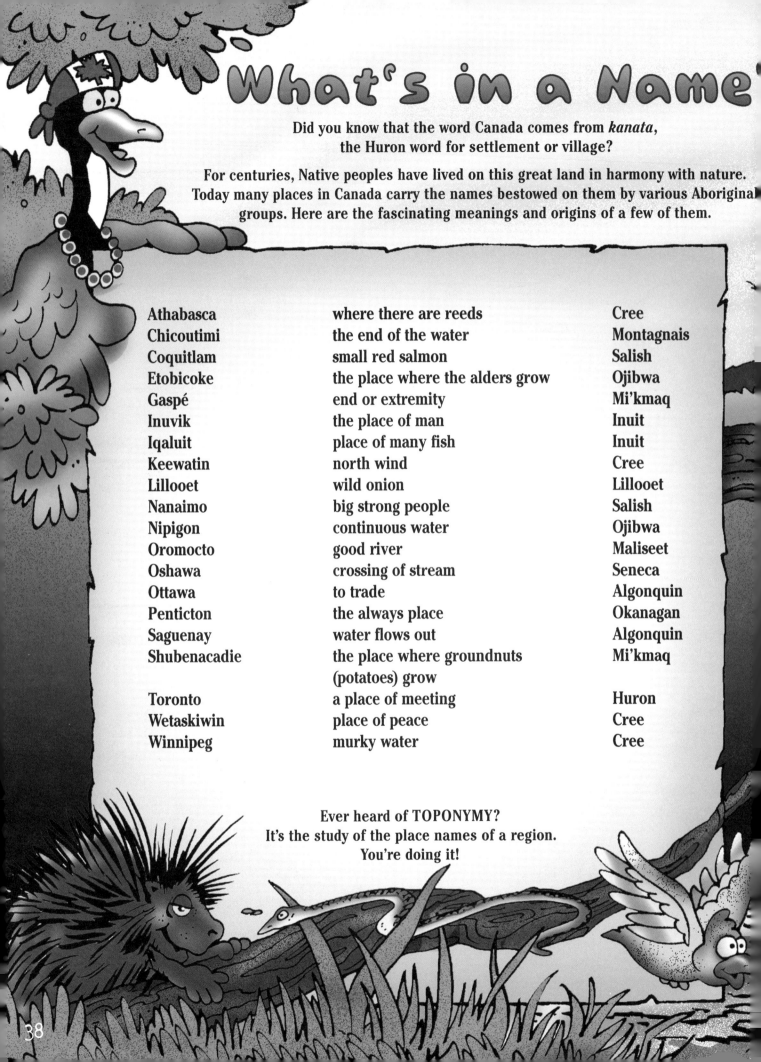

The Totally Canada Trivia Challenge Part 2

1. Which Canadian icon appears on the 1-cent coin?
   a) hockey puck   b) Stompin' Tom Connors
   c) maple leaf

2. The capital of Nunavut is . . .
   a) Iqaluit   b) Icensnow   c) Itsacold

3. Each spring, Native peoples sliced the bark of the maple tree to collect . . .
   a) marmalade   b) maple syrup
   c) their thoughts

4. What do the initials RCMP stand for?
   a) Roger Catch My Pony
   b) Royal Canadian Mounted Police
   c) Red-Coated Men in Pants

5. Which notable Canadian invented the game of basketball?
   a) James N. Smith
   b) Joey "The Shoes" Chapman
   c) James Naismith

6. Toronto's most famous landmark is . . .
   a) the CNN Tower
   b) the CN Tower
   c) 34 Webb Ave.

7. What is the English translation of the word *Lillooet*?
   a) little Louie   b) wet lily   c) wild onion

8. One of Canada's greatest contributions to sports is . . .
   a) Hockey Night in Canada
   b) Jockey Night at Woodbine
   c) Bingo Night in Oshawa

9. In September 1974, the face of the RCMP changed when . . .
   a) donut shops were banned
   b) women joined as uniformed regular members
   c) The Musical Ride opened on Broadway

10. Canadian maple syrup is also called . . .
    a) that thick, sticky, gooey stuff
    b) Bob   c) Canadian Gold

Answers on page 47

Country Canada
Total Recall

Help McKenzie Moose recall his all-Canadian roots.
Take 3 minutes to look at these 20 items that are
icons of Canadiana. Then close the book and write down as many as you
can remember. The person with the highest score is Country Canada Total
Recall Champion!

Answers on page 48

41

Candy's A-Maze-ing Maple Leaf Maze

42

It looks as though Candy the Canada Goose has one tough journey ahead of her.
She's heading south through this mixed-up maze to try to reach Ottawa by July 1st.
Use your pencil to help Candy find the best route to the finish,
so she can wave the flag on Canada Day.

Solution on page 48

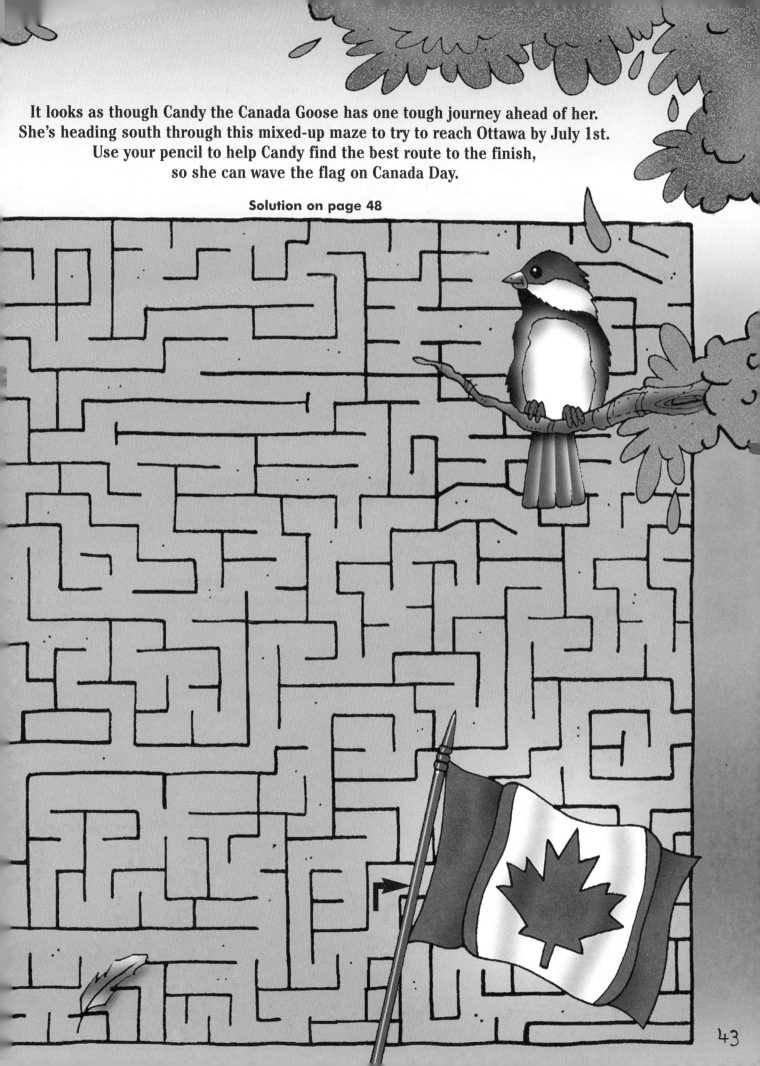

THE GAMES WE PLAY

Canada is a nation of physical activity. From jogging the rainy sea wall in Stanley Park, B.C., to sailing the salty waters off Summerside, P.E.I., Canadians are famous for their love of sports.

The Stanley Cup is the oldest trophy competed for by professional athletes in North America. It was originally donated by Frederick Arthur Stanley in 1893. Lord Stanley acquired the trophy for $50 and it was awarded every year to the amateur hockey champions of Canada. Since 1910 the Stanley Cup has become the symbol of hockey supremacy around the world.

Hockey is regarded as Canada's national sport. It is said that the word "hockey" is derived from the French word hoquet meaning shepherd's crook. As well, in Windsor, Nova Scotia, considered to be one of the birthplaces of the game, there is a story about a Colonel Hockey, who was stationed with the garrison at Fort Edward. The Colonel used the game to condition his troops and the game soon became known as Hockey's Game. Neither of these claims can be verified.

FORE! In 2003 Mike Weir became the first Canadian winner of the Masters Tournament in Augusta, Georgia. His victory also marked the first time a left-hander had won a major golf tournament in 40 years.

CANADIAN KIDS' TOP TEN SPORTS

1. soccer
2. swimming
3. hockey
4. baseball
5. basketball
6. downhill skiing
7. figure skating
8. karate
9. volleyball
10. cycling

James Naismith, born in Almonte, Ontario, invented the indoor sport of basketball in 1891. Naismith was a student, an athlete and a gym teacher at McGill University in Montreal, Quebec. He went on to teach physical education in the United States for many years. In 1959 James Naismith was inducted into the Basketball Hall of Fame that now bears his name.

ANSWERS

The Maple Leaf Flag (p. 5)
Canada, red, leaf, sugar, twice, Flag

Sea-to-Sea Scavenger Hunt (p. 6)
1. campfire — pp. 20, 28
2. Saddledome — p. 33
3. bunch of wheat — p. 40
4. Albertosaurus dinosaur — p. 14
5. moose in a Mountie hat — p. 32
6. pine cone — pp. 12, 48
7. Parliament Buildings — p. 13
8. goalie stick — p. 30
9. porcupine — p. 38
10. turkey on rye — p. 21
11. snapping turtle — p. 28
12. maple leaf mug — p. 12
13. beaver on a totem pole — p. 45
14. bear with a toothache — p. 28
15. hot air balloon — pp. 2, 3
16. Canadian quarter — p. 27
17. octopus — pp. 30, 31
18. lobster in a box — p. 6
19. bucket of fish — p. 8
20. Canada goose holding a flag —
    pp. 4, 15

Canada Quiz (p. 6)
Lake Michigan

Famous Canadians (p. 7)
1. Jacques Cartier
2. Sir John A. Macdonald
3. Dr. Frederick Banting
4. Terry Fox
5. Roberta Bondar

Wet 'n' Wild Hink Pinks (p. 8)
1. Cod Fraud
2. Whale Sale
3. Dull Gull
4. Squid's Kids
5. Brave Wave
6. Wet Net
7. Squish Fish
8. Seal Meal
9. Clam Jam
10. Crab Flab

Country-Wide Word Scramble (p. 9)
1. ROBERT MUNSCH
2. PABLUM
3. ROCKY MOUNTAINS
4. PIERRE TRUDEAU
5. GREAT LAKES
6. MAPLE LEAF
7. SNOWMOBILE
8. ST. LAWRENCE RIVER
9. PRINCE EDWARD ISLAND
10. BEAVER
11. MOUNT LOGAN
12. CARIBOU
13. INUIT
14. GREEN GABLES
15. MCGILL UNIVERSITY
16. MAPLE SYRUP
17. RCMP
18. SASKATCHEWAN
19. SAMUEL DE
    CHAMPLAIN
20. STANLEY CUP

Crazy Canada (p. 12)
1. platypus (Australia)
2. Swiss Army knife
   (Switzerland)
3. great white shark
   (New Zealand)
4. Stars and Stripes
   (United States)
5. pineapple (Hawaii)
6. Union Jack (United
   Kingdom)
7. jaguar (South America)
8. elephant (Africa)
9. blowfish (Japan)
10. bananas (Panama)

Barky Beaver's Ottawa Expedition (p. 13)

Can You Spot McKenzie Moose?
(p. 10-11)
He is looking at the bird.
(p. 11)

Canada Quiz (p. 10)
45%

Canada Quiz (p. 14-15)
Lester B. Pearson

Totally Canada Picture Riddles (p. 16)

1. Ottawa
2. Chicoutimi
3. Manitoba
4. Nunavut
5. Lunenburg
6. Medicine Hat
7. Penticton
8. Labrador

All Canadian Criss-Cross (p. 17)

1. Kingston
2. Owen Sound
3. Rocky Mountain House
4. Edmonton
5. Floral
6. Napanee
7. White Rock
8. Chatsworth
9. Parry Sound
10. St. Boniface
11. Quebec City
12. St. John's

Metric Mania (p. 19)

1. a) 32°C
2. c) 82.5 L
3. a) 10 kg
4. b) 50 cm
5. b) 4 L
6. a) 400 kg
7. c) 1.6 sq m

Canada Quiz (p. 19)

One: British Columbia

Do You C What I C? (p. 20)

1. Cabbage
2. Cake
3. Calculator
4. Calendar
5. Camel
6. Camera
7. Campfire
8. Can
9. Canada goose
10. Candies
11. Candle
12. Cat
13. Chair
14. Clock
15. Coins
16. Comb
17. Compass
18. Cookies
19. Cork
20. Corn
21. Cow
22. Crab
23. Crow
24. Cup
25. Curling rock

Get Cookin' Canada! (p. 21)

1. British Columbia / D
2. Alberta / B, D
3. Yukon / A, B, C, D
4. Nunavut / A, B, C, D
5. Ontario / A, D
6. Manitoba / B, D
7. Saskatchewan / A, B
8. Quebec / D
9. New Brunswick / B
10. Nova Scotia / B, C
11. Newfoundland and Labrador / B, D
12. P.E.I. / B, C
13. Northwest Territories / B, C

Canada Quiz (p. 22)

A lion and a unicorn

The Totally Canada Trivia Challenge – Part 1 (p. 23)

1. b) macaroni and cheese
2. c) the True North strong and free
3. a) Flag Day
4. c) Farley Mowat
5. b) 5 points
6. c) Napanee
7. a) ginger ale
8. a) annual snowfall
9. c) Al Capone
10. b) in metric

Totally Canada Crossword (p. 24)

Across	Down
3. Canadian Gold	1. white
7. beaver	2. Parry Sound
8. Estevan	4. maple leaf
9. antlers	5. basketball
10. last	6. hockey
11. Bateman	11. Bishop
14. Cartier	12. Ottawa
17. Weir	13. America
19. Inuit	15. toonie
20. cheese	16. metric
21. Ride	18. Quebec

Canada Quiz (p. 25)

c) a softball

Kooky Canuck Alphabet Adventure (p. 26)

1. TERRY FOX
2. SHANIA TWAIN
3. ROBERT BATEMAN
4. MARTIN BRODEUR
5. MONCTON
6. QUEBEC CITY
7. MANITOBA
8. NUNAVUT
9. NEWFOUNDLAND
10. TIMMINS
11. BACK BACON
12. ALBERTOSAURUS
13. BASKETBALL
14. CANOE
15. POLAR BEAR
16. GINGER ALE
17. ICE HOCKEY
18. BLUE JAY
19. NANAIMO BAR
20. INUKSUK

Hidden Message: (p. 26)

CANADA RULES

Funny Money (p. 27)

1) $20 2) $100 3) $5 4) $10
5) $50 6) two maple leaves
7) a beaver 8) the schooner Bluenose
9) a caribou 10) a loon
11) a polar bear

Take a Hike Hinkie Pinkies (p. 28)
1. Beaver Cleaver
2. Snapper Rapper
3. Hermit Permit
4. Lazy Daisy
5. Polar Molar
6. Jerky Turkey
7. Mountain Fountain
8. Bugless Douglas

Canada Quiz (p. 28)
the Mackenzie River

Spot the Differences (p. 30-31)
1. Eagle-eyed fan has removed his earmuffs
2. Pucks have disappeared from the goal crease
3. Octopus is missing a tentacle
4. Referee has swallowed his whistle
5. Player #3 has changed his jersey to #11
6. Player #66 has bandaged his face
7. Bird has grabbed a hockey stick from the bench
8. Moose's goalie sweater emblem is now a "C"
9. Polar bear fan has lost his watch
10. Snowflakes are falling

Coast-to-Coast Canadian Landmarks (p. 33)
1. Canada Place — British Columbia
2. Saddledome — Alberta
3. Citadel Clock — Nova Scotia
4. Chateau Frontenac — Quebec
5. Green Gables — Prince Edward Island
6. Confederation Bridge — New Brunswick AND P.E.I.
7. CN Tower — Ontario

Know Your Capitals, Eh! (p. 36-37)
1. Whitehorse
2. Yellowknife
3. Iqaluit
4. Victoria
5. Edmonton
6. Regina
7. Winnipeg
8. Toronto
9. Quebec City
10. Fredericton
11. Halifax
12. Charlottetown
13. St. John's

The Totally Canada Trivia Challenge – Part 2 (p. 39)
1. c) maple leaf
2. a) Iqaluit
3. b) maple syrup
4. b) Royal Canadian Mounted Police
5. c) James Naismith
6. b) the CN Tower
7. c) wild onion
8. a) Hockey Night in Canada
9. b) Women joined as uniformed regular members
10. c) Canadian Gold

Canada-Wide Word Search (p. 34-35)

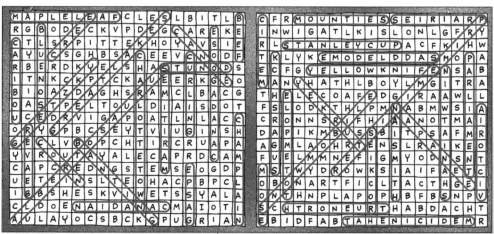

Country Canada Total Recall (p. 40-41)

1. polar bear
2. salmon
3. Canadian flag
4. corn
5. map of Canada
6. Mountie hat
7. pancakes and maple syrup
8. CN Tower
9. beluga whale
10. inuksuk
11. hockey stick
12. lighthouse
13. Canada geese
14. Rocky Mountains
15. forests
16. wheat
17. lobster
18. beaver
19. Nanaimo bars
20. maple leaf

Candy's A-MAZE-ING Maple Leaf Maze (p. 42-43)

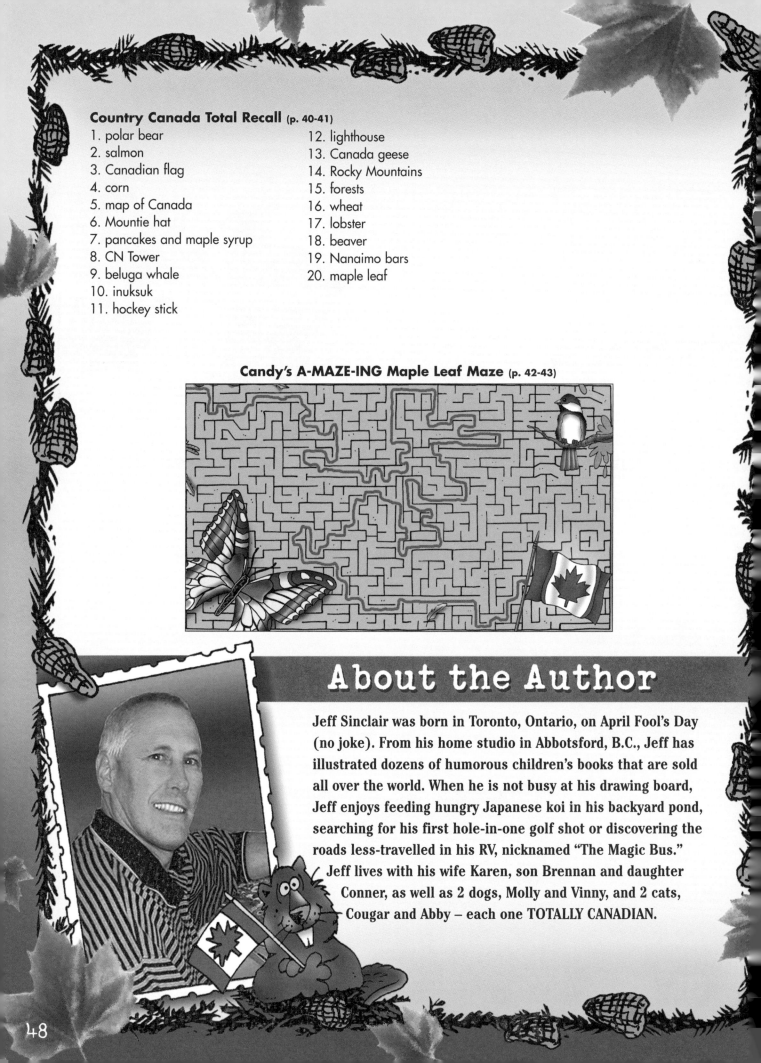

About the Author

Jeff Sinclair was born in Toronto, Ontario, on April Fool's Day (no joke). From his home studio in Abbotsford, B.C., Jeff has illustrated dozens of humorous children's books that are sold all over the world. When he is not busy at his drawing board, Jeff enjoys feeding hungry Japanese koi in his backyard pond, searching for his first hole-in-one golf shot or discovering the roads less-travelled in his RV, nicknamed "The Magic Bus." Jeff lives with his wife Karen, son Brennan and daughter Conner, as well as 2 dogs, Molly and Vinny, and 2 cats, Cougar and Abby – each one TOTALLY CANADIAN.